The Alphabet
Animal Book

Young & Gifted Series

THIS BOOK BELONGS TO:

_____

Aardvark
A

The name aardvark is Afrikaans for "earth pig."
Their diet consists almost entirely of ants
and termites. Aardvarks are found throughout
much of sub-Saharan Africa.

Bear
B

Black bears are not always black in color. They can be black, brown, cinnamon, blond, blue-gray, or white. There are eight bear species in the world.

Cheetah
C

Cheetahs are the fastest land animal with a speed between 50 to 80 miles per hour. The name cheetah comes from a Hindi word, chita, meaning spotted one.

Donkey
D

A donkey can live close to 50 years. They are also very intelligent and strong. A donkey is actually stronger than a horse of the same size.

Elephant
E

Elephants are the world's largest land animal. There are three species of elephants: African Savanna, African Forest and Asian and you can tell them apart by their ear shapes.

Fox
F

Foxes are nocturnal, sleeping generally throughout the day and up at night. They can make 40 different sounds. A male fox is called a dog and a female fox is called a vixen.

Giraffe
G

Giraffes are the tallest mammal in the world. Each giraffe has its own unique coat pattern with no two being the same. It is like human fingerprints.

Hippopotamus
H

Even though Hippopotamus is the third largest mammal on earth, they are herbivores (plant eaters). Hippos skin produce a natural sun-block.

Iguana

I

Iguanas can shed their tails and skin when necessary. Green Iguanas have three eyes. Their third eye is called the pineal gland or parietal eye.

Jellyfish

J

Jellyfish are the oldest multicellular animals on the planet. Jellyfish don't have a brain, heart, lungs or blood. They absorb oxygen through their thin skin.

Kangaroo
K

The name Kangaroo comes the Aboriginal Guugu Yimithirr language. Kangaroos can't hop or walk backwards. Kangaroos are the largest marsupials on earth.

Lion

L

Lions can eat around a quarter of their body weight. Lions are the laziest of the big cats, spending up to 20 hours of the day resting or sleeping.

Monkey
M

Monkeys communicate with each other by using facial expressions, body movements, and noises. Mandrills are the largest monkey in the world.

Narwhal

N

Narwhals can live up to 50 years. Their protruding tusk is actually a tooth and are most commonly found only on males.

Owl

O

Owls are nocturnal which means they are awake at night. An owls claws are called Talons and they are used to help catch their prey. There are more than 200 species of owls.

Penguin
P

Penguins are aquatic, flightless birds. Penguins eat krill, squids, and fish. They don't have teeth so they use their Bills to help them eat.

Quail
Q

Quails eat seeds, grain and insects. Even though they have wings, they can only fly short distances.

Raccoon
R

Raccoons are nocturnal animals and rarely seen during the day. The have excellent night vision. Raccoons have dexterous hands and can open up cans and bottles.

Squirrel
S

Squirrels are considered herbivores (plant eaters) but they also eat insects such as butterflies, caterpillars, and larvae. Some squirrels fly which is actually a glide.

Tiger

T

Tigers are the largest wild cats in the world. The are meat eaters which makes them carnivores. Tigers are mostly nocturnal which means they are awake at night.

Urchin
U

Urchins live in all 5 oceans. Sea Urchins have hundreds of feet. Sea Urchins are omnivores who eat everything from kelp to sea cucumbers.

Vulture
V

Vultures are carnivores (meat eaters) and have an excellent sense of sight and smell to help them locate food. There are 23 species of vulture.

Wolf

W

The wolf is a large canine native to Eurasia and North America. There are two distinct species of wolf residing in North America, the gray wolf and the red wolf. The wolf have 42 teeth.

Xenops
X

Xenops are small with relatively long tails. Xenops are found in rain forests in South and Central America and Mexico. They eat insects which they find on bark, stumps and twigs.

Yak

Y

Yaks have two stomachs that help them successfully get all the nutrients out of the plants they eat. They are very strong animals and can carry up to 150 pounds on their backs.

Zebra
Z

Zebras are herbivores (plant eaters) who can sleep standing up. A zebras stripes are unique to them like a humans fingerprints. No two zebras stripes are exactly alike.